ULTIMATE
SLIME
SCHOOL

© 2017 Weldon Owen, a part of
Kings Road Publishing
Part of Bonnier Publishing
Suite 3.08 The Plaza, 535 King's Road,
London SW10 0SZ, UK
www.bonnierpublishing.co.uk

Publisher: Donna Gregory
Project Editor: Matt Yeo
Writer: Laura Baker
Designer: Darren Jordan
Packaged by Cloud King Creative
Proofreading and technical notes: Steph
    Sykes, SlimeyWimeyStuff on Instagram
Americanization: Kris Hirschmann

A big thank you to PastelSlimesUK owner
Abigael Longfellow for all of her amazing
help with creating this book! For more of Abi's
totally brilliant slimes, go to www.instagram.
com/pastelslimesuk.

Certain photographs used in this publication
are used by license or permission from the
owner thereof, or are otherwise publicly
available. This publication is not endorsed by
any person or entity appearing herein. Any
product names, logos, brands, or trademarks
featured or referred to in the publication are
the property of their respective trademark
owners. Use of these names and images does
not imply any responsibility, cooperation or
endorsement.

ISBN: 978-1-7834-2475-7

Printed in China

10 9 8 7 6 5 4 3 2 1

IMPORTANT SAFETY NOTES:
The activities in these books involve lots
of different ingredients. Some people
may have sensitivities to certain ingredients,
so we always advise always wearing gloves
when making slime. Like any activity, adult
supervision is required – adults should always
handle all ingredients involving chemicals.
It is also advised that old clothing is worn,
and any surfaces are carefully covered to
prevent damage. Always disinfect and wash
all tools and areas used once you have
finished, and under no circumstance ingest
any of the slime, unless the recipe explicitly
states that it is safe to do so.

ULTIMATE
SLIME
SCHOOL

CONTENT

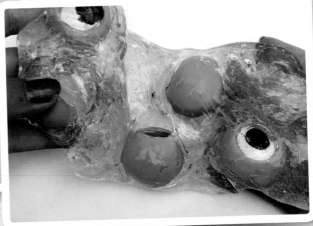

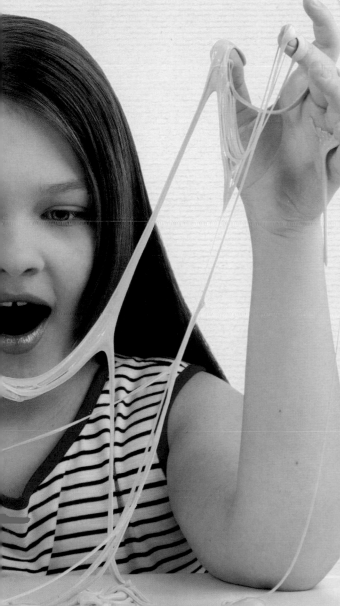

What is SLIME?

Slime is the super-cool, super-squishy, super-stretchy trend you just have to try for yourself.

- ✹ Slime may ooze through your fingers like a liquid or bounce like a solid. If you pull it slowly, it will stretch, but if you pull it too hard, it will snap. Slime is science in action!

- ✹ DIY slime is something you can make at home with things you can find around the house, plus a few special items. There are lots of slime variations you can try, and even some science experiments too.

- ✹ When you get it right, a ball of slime is super satisfying to play with. Poke, fold, and squish the slime to relieve stress, help with anxiety, or just feel good.

SLIME SAFETY

Before we get started, let's go over some ground rules to make sure your slime-making time is both fun and safe.

- Most slime is not edible. Do not eat it!
- Wash your hands well after making slime to make sure nothing gets in your eyes.
- Clean your work surfaces afterward too.
- Make sure you are using safe ingredients, such as white glue. Read the labels of your ingredients to get to know their safety instructions.
- Keep slime away from carpets, upholstery, and absorbent materials.
- Young children should always be supervised when making or handling any type of slime.
- Keep slime away from animals.
- Always have an adult at home when making slime, just in case something goes wrong.

SLIME-MAKING INGREDIENTS

1 The base

Most slime recipes start with one basic ingredient:

Glue: Look for white, clear, or even glitter-type school glue. White glue is the most common, but be aware that it will absorb some of the color you add. Clear glue will show any extras you add very clearly and needs less activator. Glitter glue has extras built in! Make sure whatever glue you choose has the ingredient Polyvinyl acetate.

2 The color (optional)

You can leave your slime the color of your glue, or you can turn it into any color you like using an additive:

Food coloring (liquid or gel): You just need a small drop for your color to pop.

Acrylic paint: This offers a huge range of colors to choose from.

3 The add-ons (optional)

You can add all sorts of things into your slime for texture and decoration, such as:

Glitter: Add some sparkle with one or multiple colors of glitter.

Styrofoam balls: These will create what's called "floam."

Beads: Try different shapes and colors for different looks and feels.

There are endless types of slime you can create by combining different variations of key ingredients. Mix, match, and make!

Science Alert!

Slime turns from liquid into goo when a glue ingredient called PVA (Polyvinyl acetate) comes into contact with sodium borate, sodium tetraborate, or disodium tetraborate, so your activator needs to have one of these in its listed ingredients.

4 The finish (optional)

Different ingredients will create different slime textures and finishes:

Lotion: Adding a liquid lotion will make your slime extra stretchy.

Baby oil: This makes your slime super shiny.

Baby powder: Dust some powder into the mix for a matte (non-shiny) finish.

Liquid candle or soap scents: Add an aroma to your slime with a drop or two of a crafting scent.

5 The activator

Every slime recipe needs an activator to turn the liquid mixture into the squishy goo that you're after. Try any of these once you have all your other ingredients in place, and see which works best for you:

Liquid laundry detergent containing boric acid

Liquid starch

Contact solution

Baking soda

TOP TIP!

Add in your activator a little at a time. Mix really well with a spoon between additions until the mixture starts to turn into slime. Then start kneading with your hands.

11

SLIME-MAKING TOOLS AND TIPS

For every slime recipe, you'll need a mixing bowl and a spoon. Find a clear, clean work surface and wash your hands before getting started.

Each finished slime should keep for a couple of weeks if stored properly. Follow these tips to keep it as fresh as possible:

Spoon

Clean work surface

Mixing bowl

- Store slime in an airtight container.
- Add more activator if needed when you take out your slime again.
- Knead and fold your slime every now and then to keep it flexible.

Some things to note:

- Slime is not an exact science. The quality of ingredients and temperature of the room can impact how it works. Play around with quantity to find what works best for you. Test different ingredients too.

- Be patient! Some slimes require a lot of mixing and kneading to turn into the right consistency. Add small amounts of activator at a time and keep on mixing.

- Slime will soften with the heat of your hand.

- Remember that your slime is homemade, so don't expect it to feel as firm as putty that you would buy in a store.

BASIC SLIME WITH LAUNDRY DETERGENT

Start with a basic slime to get a feel for the process and an understanding of how the different ingredients work to create your goo. This recipe uses three simple ingredients from home.

YOU WILL NEED

Liquid laundry detergent

Food coloring

18 ounces (500 ml) white or clear glue

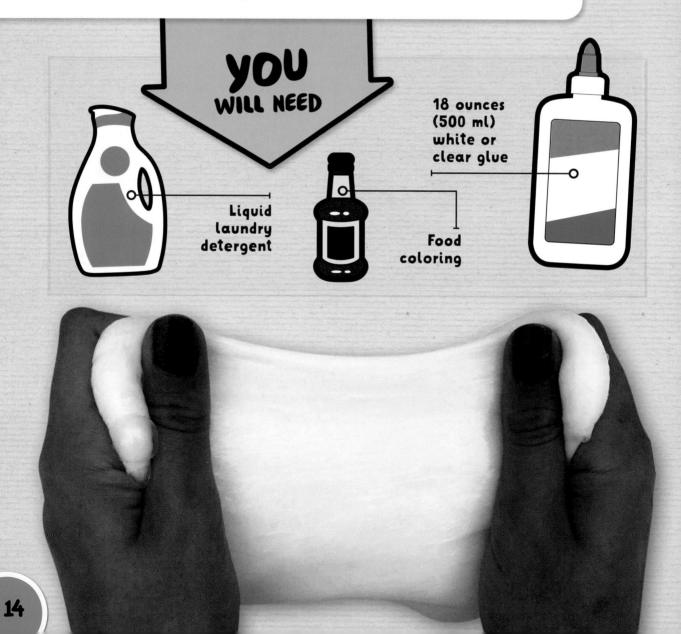

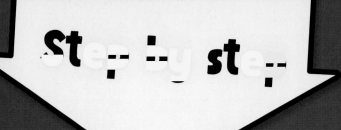

step by step

1 Pour the glue into a large mixing bowl. Add some drops of food coloring and mix well with a spoon. Add more food coloring if needed to get the color desired.

2 Add a small dash of laundry detergent and mix well. Continue mixing in small amounts of laundry detergent until the mixture starts to come off the sides of the bowl.

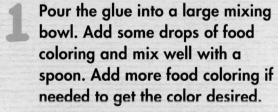

3 Use your hands to knead the mixture for at least five minutes, until it turns into a slime consistency (solid, stretchy, and not sticking to your fingers).

TOP TIP!
Many slime recipes don't have perfect measurements. Add small amounts of ingredients at a time to find what works for you.

BASIC SLIME WITH CONTACT SOLUTION

Step it up by trying a different activator. If you don't have contact solution, try this recipe with baking soda only.

YOU WILL NEED

Contact solution

Baby oil

18 ounces (500 ml) white or clear glue

½ tsp (4 g) baking soda

Food coloring or acrylic paint

TOP TIP!
Clear glue is a different consistency than white glue and doesn't need as much activator to turn into slime.

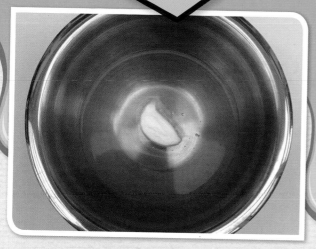

1 Pour the glue into a large mixing bowl. Add the baking soda and mix well with a spoon.

2 Add a few drops of food coloring or a squirt of paint. Mix gently until well combined and the color that you want your slime to be.

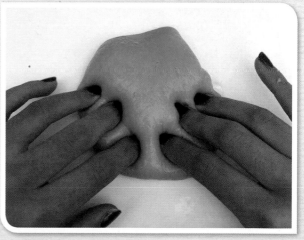

3 Add the contact solution one squirt at a time, mixing it in well between squirts.

4 When the slime stops sticking to the sides of the bowl, add a few drops of baby oil and knead this in well. This makes the slime less sticky and more stretchy.

FLUFFY SLIME

Fluffy slime is...well, fluffy! It uses shaving foam to give it a light feel with plenty of volume.

YOU WILL NEED

Food coloring or acrylic paint

18 ounces (500 ml) white or clear glue

Liquid laundry detergent

½ cup (120 ml) shaving foam

TOP TIP!
Don't add too much laundry detergent or the mixture will become too rubbery and will snap instead of stretch.

Step by step

1 Pour the glue into a large mixing bowl. Add the shaving foam and fold it in gently.

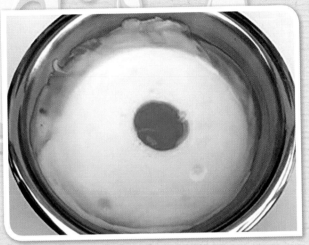

2 Add some drops of food coloring or a squirt of paint. Mix gently until well combined and the color that you want your slime to be.

3 Add a small dash of laundry detergent and mix well. Continue mixing in small amounts of laundry detergent until the mixture starts to come off the sides of the bowl.

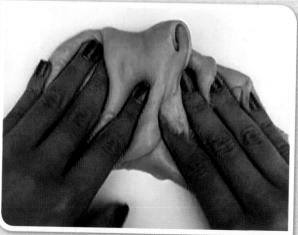

4 Use your hands to knead the slime mixture until it turns into a slime consistency. Do this gently on this slime to keep its volume.

CRUNCHY SLIME

Listen to the crackle and crunch of this noisy slime as you squish it around in your fingers. Super satisfying for the hands and ears!

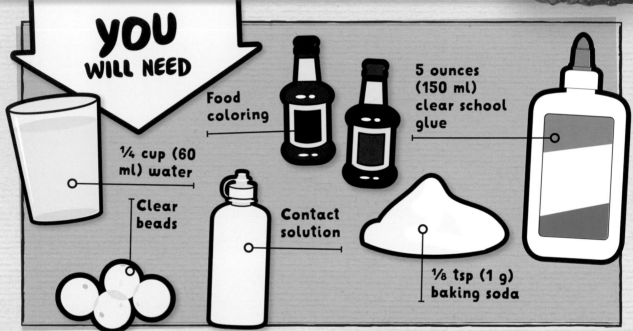

YOU WILL NEED

Food coloring

5 ounces (150 ml) clear school glue

¼ cup (60 ml) water

Clear beads

Contact solution

⅛ tsp (1 g) baking soda

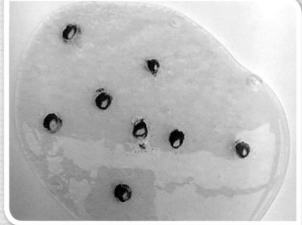

1 Pour the clear glue into a large mixing bowl. Add the water and mix well with a spoon.

2 Add some drops of food coloring. Mix gently until well combined and the color that you want your slime to be.

Step by step

TOP TIP!
Try making this slime in lots of different colors for a rainbow selection of crunch-tastic stress relief.

3 Add the baking soda and mix well.

4 Pour enough beads into the bowl to cover the top of your slime. Mix them into your slime.

5 Add a few squirts of contact solution. Mix well with a spoon until the mixture turns into a slime texture. Use your hands to knead the slime and get it all off the sides of the bowl.

6 For extra crunch, pour more clear beads into a bowl, then place your slime on top. The beads will stick to the slime. Pick it up and knead it all together. Hear the crunch!

GLITTER SLIME

This is the sparkliest slime there is. Choose a base glitter color and then add a complement to it for depth. For example, add some light blue glitter to give depth to a dark blue mix, or add some gold glitter to add a touch of luxury to a sparkly pink slime.

YOU WILL NEED

¼ cup (60 ml) water

5 ounces (150 ml) clear school glue

Glitter (2-3 shades are best)

Contact solution

step by step

TOP TIP!
Clear glue is best for glitter slime, allowing the glitter to sparkle in the transparent mixture.

1 Pour the clear glue into a large mixing bowl. Add the water and mix well with a spoon.

2 Sprinkle your glitter across the top of your slime. Mix it in and add more if you want. Be generous!

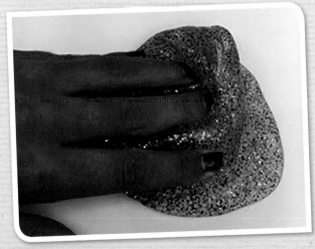

Extra Stuff

Try this recipe with beads instead of glitter for a cool and personalized look.

3 Add a few squirts of contact solution. Mix well with a spoon until the mixture turns into a slime texture. Use your hands to knead the slime and get it all off the sides of the bowl.

METALLIC SLIME

Shiny happy slime! Add a metallic finish to your slime by using a special type of paint.

YOU WILL NEED

¼ cup (60 ml) water

Metallic acrylic paint

Liquid laundry detergent

18 ounces (500 ml) clear glue

1 Pour the clear glue into a large mixing bowl. Add the water and mix well with a spoon.

2 Add a few squirts of the metallic paint and mix in well. Add more until the mixture is the color that you'd like.

3 Add a small dash of laundry detergent and mix well. Continue mixing in small amounts of laundry detergent until the mixture starts to come off the sides of the bowl.

4 Use your hands to knead the slime mixture until it turns into a slime consistency.

25

FLUFFY FLOAM

This slime doubles up the foam, making it super light and satisfying. Squeeze this and feel your stresses float away.

YOU WILL NEED

Liquid laundry detergent

White or colored small foam balls

18 ounces (500 ml) white or clear glue

½ cup (120 ml) shaving foam

TOP TIP!

Make sure to use a very large bowl for this recipe. Foam pieces can easily jump out and go everywhere!

Step by step

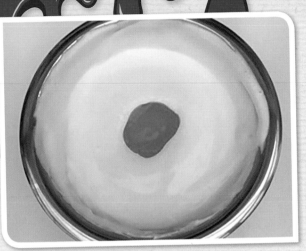

1 Pour the glue into a large mixing bowl. Add the shaving foam and fold it in gently.

2 Add a small dash of laundry detergent and mix well. Continue mixing in small amounts of laundry detergent until the mixture starts to come off the sides of the bowl.

3 Use your hands to knead the slime mixture until it turns into a slime consistency. Lift the slime out of the bowl.

4 Place the foam pieces into the bottom of the bowl and your slime on top. Squish and fold the pieces into the slime until it's all combined.

SQUISHY FLOUR SLIME

This slime uses only edible ingredients from the kitchen, so it's nice and safe, and satisfyingly squishy too.

YOU WILL NEED

1 cup (240 ml) water

9 tbsp (150 g) table salt

2 tbsp (30 ml) cooking oil

2 cups (240 g) flour

Step by step

TOP TIP!
You can sprinkle glitter, sequins, or beads onto the finished dough and knead it in for some extra bling.

1 Place the flour, salt, and oil in a large mixing bowl.

2 Add the water and mix with a spoon until well combined and until the dough starts to come off the sides of the bowl.

3 Use your hands to knead the dough into a squishy ball.

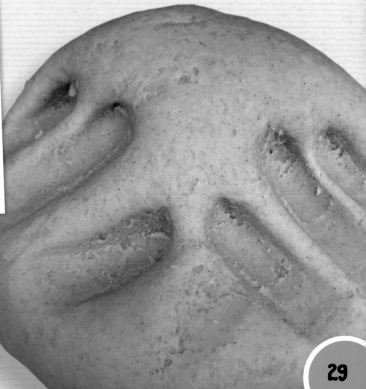

RAINBOW SLIME

Also known as unicorn poop slime, this colorful concoction is beautiful and squishy at the same time.

YOU WILL NEED

White fluffy slime (see pages 18-19)

Lots of food coloring or acrylic paint

TOP TIP!
Be careful not to overmix the colors, or you'll end up with a lump of gray slime.

1 Make a large recipe of white fluffy slime.

2 Divide the slime into equal parts of as many colors as you'd like in your rainbow. Add a drop of food coloring or paint to each section of white slime. Knead the color in carefully, one slime at a time, until you have a rainbow selection of slime. You may need to wash your hands between colors.

3 Roll out long sausage shapes of each slime. Place all the colors together and gently press.

4 Stretch the combined slime for a stripy rainbow look, or really go for it and mix it all together to make cool patterns.

MILKSHAKE SLIME

Display your slime like a real pro with this fancy finish. Just remember it isn't actually edible!

YOU WILL NEED

A clear plastic cup or ice cream sundae glass

Fluffy slime (see pages 18-19)

1 straw (optional)

Shaving foam

Small colored foam balls (optional)

st p by st p

1 Make a batch of fluffy slime in whatever color you'd like your milkshake to be.

2 Squeeze the slime into the plastic cup or sundae glass, right up to the brim. Let it settle.

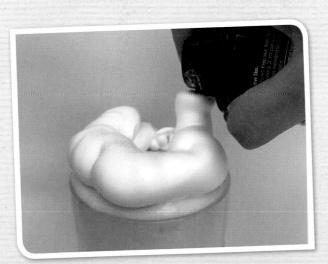

3 Swirl shaving foam on top. If you want, stick in a straw and sprinkle some small colored foam balls on top of the shaving foam as decoration. Beautiful!

BUTTER SLIME

Butter slime is as smooth as...butter! Use modeling clay, which you can buy online, to give it a super-smooth texture like no other slime. You can even spread this slime with a knife!

YOU WILL NEED

1 cup (240 ml) white glue

18 ounces (500 g) modeling clay

1 tsp (7 g) baking soda

Yellow food coloring or acrylic paint

1 cup (240 ml) shaving foam

1 Pour the glue into a large mixing bowl. Add the shaving foam and mix well with a spoon.

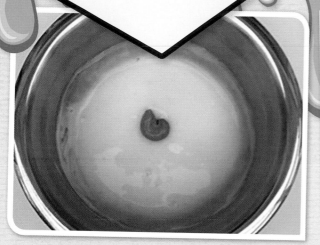

2 Add a few drops of the yellow food coloring or a squirt of paint and mix in well.

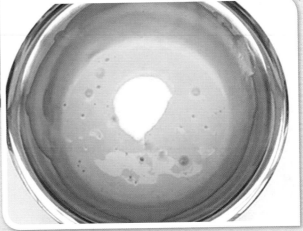

3 Mix in the baking soda.

4 Add a few squirts of contact solution. Mix well with a spoon until the mixture turns into a slime texture. Use your hands to knead the slime and get it all off the sides of the bowl.

5 Tear off a chunk of modeling clay about the size of your palm. Place it on top of your yellow slime and start folding it in, mixing it all together well. You should feel the texture of your slime change to butter-like!

ICEBERG SLIME

Find out what's under the tip of the iceberg...
This slime has a crazy crunch on top and a
hidden gooey layer underneath. Super cool!

YOU WILL NEED

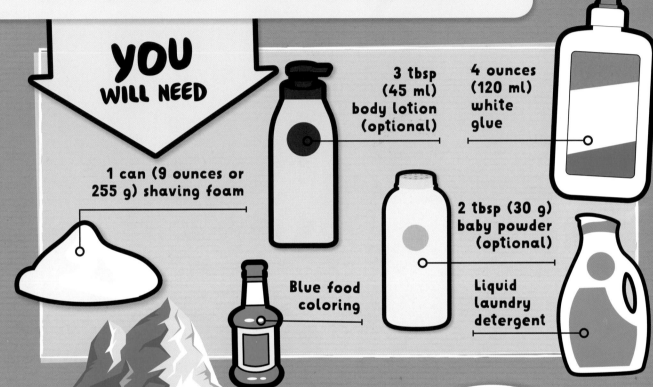

1 can (9 ounces or 255 g) shaving foam

3 tbsp (45 ml) body lotion (optional)

4 ounces (120 ml) white glue

2 tbsp (30 g) baby powder (optional)

Blue food coloring

Liquid laundry detergent

TOP TIP!

You can mix the crunchy top layer back into the slime and let it sit out again if you want to recreate the iceberg after you've played with it.

TOP TIP!
Put the slime in the fridge for the third day for extra top-level crunch. Brrr-illiant!

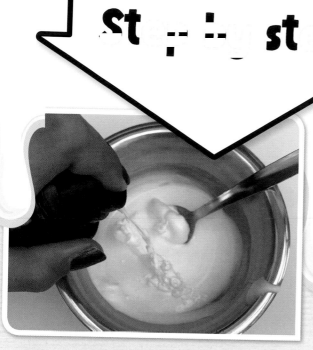

1 Pour the glue into a large mixing bowl. Add all the shaving foam and mix well with a spoon. This might take a while!

2 Add the body lotion for stretch and the baby powder for a matte look. Add a generous amount of the blue food coloring and mix this all together well.

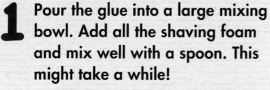

3 Add a small dash of laundry detergent and mix well. Continue mixing in small amounts of laundry detergent until the mixture starts to come off the sides of the bowl. Use your hands to knead it into a slime consistency. This takes patience since this is a big slime!

4 Pat the slime down into the bowl so it lies flat. Let it sit out uncovered for two to three days. The top layer should turn solid—but if you crack through, you'll find gooey slime below!

MAGNETIC SLIME

This slime will eat up anything (magnetic) in its path. Add iron filings, which you can buy online, and then use a strong magnet to see how the slime reacts. Slime attraction!

YOU WILL NEED

9 tbsp (150 g) iron filings

18 ounces (500 ml) white or clear glue

Liquid laundry detergent

½ cup (120 ml) shaving foam

Silver or gold glitter

Try This!

Hold a strong magnet near the slime and watch a finger of slime reach out toward the magnet. Or, put a strong magnet at the end of the slime and let go. If your magnets are strong enough, the slime will consume the magnet!

1 Pour the glue into a large mixing bowl. Add the shaving foam and fold it in gently.

Step by step

TOP TIP!
Add more iron filings for a stronger magnetic pull.

2 Add the iron filings. Mix well with a spoon.

3 Add the glitter. Mix well with a spoon.

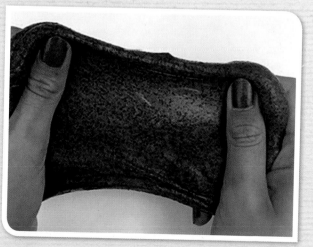

4 Add a small dash of laundry detergent and mix well. Continue mixing in small amounts of laundry detergent until the mixture starts to come off the sides of the bowl.

5 Use your hands to knead the slime mixture until it turns into a slime consistency.

EYEBALL SLIME

You'll feel like you're being watched with this sticky, gooey, spooky slime... Mix it up and let it ooze from your fingers. Mwah ha ha!

YOU WILL NEED

4 cups (about 1 liter) water

8 ounces (240 ml) clear glue

1 pack eyeball beads or sticky eyeballs

Liquid laundry detergent

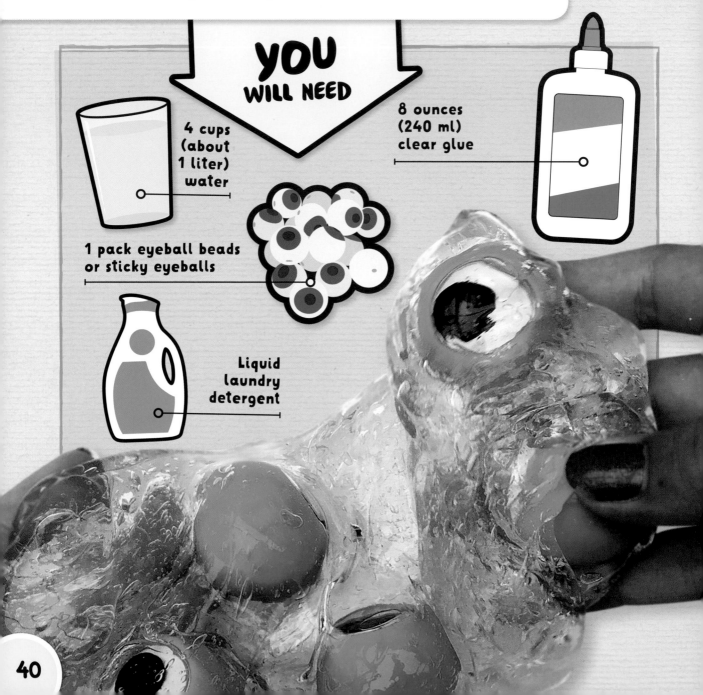

Step by step

1 Pour the water into a large mixing bowl. Add the clear glue and mix well.

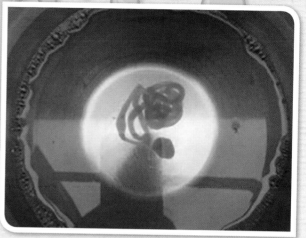

2 Add a small dash of laundry detergent and mix well. When the mixture starts sticking together, use your hands to squeeze and knead it into a slime. This spooky slime will be stickier and messier than others in this book.

3 Drop the eyeballs onto your slime and mix them in with your hands.

41

MELTING SNOWMAN SLIME

See a poor snowman melt before your very eyes!

YOU WILL NEED

1 cup (240 ml) water

1 cup (240 ml) liquid starch

1 cup (240 ml) white glue

White, silver, or light blue glitter

Snowman decorations (foam pieces, buttons, etc.)

1 In a large bowl, mix the white glue and water together well.

step by step

Try This!
Instead of step 4, mold the slime into a snowman shape. Hold it in place while you add the snowman features. Then take your hands away and watch your snowman melt!

2 Mix in glitter. Add the color and amount that you'd like for your snowman.

3 Pour in the liquid starch. Stir with a spoon until the mixture becomes too firm to do so. Then knead with your hands for a few minutes until the mixture turns into slime. Let the mixture set for 15 minutes.

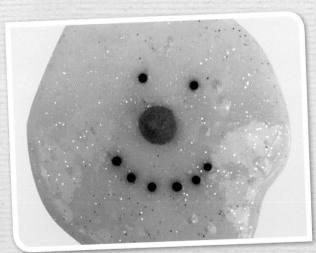

4 Lay the slime on the table. Add your snowman parts and you'll have a snowman puddle to play with!

EDIBLE CANDY SLIME

This slime is satisfying AND delicious. It's totally safe and super sweet, if you feel like sampling your work. Just make sure you wash your hands before you make it!

YOU WILL NEED

Powdered sugar

Box of colored soft taffy candy

1 Unwrap the soft taffy candies and place them in a bowl. You could choose to separate the colors that work well together, such as orange and yellow, and red and pink.

2 Ask an adult to boil a pot of shallow water on the stove. Using an oven mitt, place the bowl inside the pot. Stir with a spoon until the candy melts completely. Using an oven mitt, take the bowl out of the water and turn off the stove.

3 While the candy cools, dust powdered sugar over a clean cutting board or mat. When the mixture is cool enough to handle, scrape it out of the bowl onto the powdered sugar.

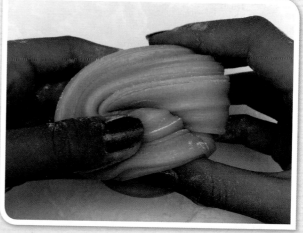

4 Knead in the powdered sugar and add more to thicken your slime.

EDIBLE CHOCOLATE SLIME

For chocoholic slime-oholics! This is another slime you can take a bite out of, if you've made it with clean hands.

YOU WILL NEED

Powdered sugar

14 ounces (396 g) sweetened condensed milk

Cornstarch

4 ounces (110 g) plain chocolate, broken into squares

Science Alert!

The cornstarch acts as a thickener and your activator in this recipe, turning the mixture from liquid to moldable slime.

TOP TIP!
This slime will keep in a sealed container in the fridge for a few days only.

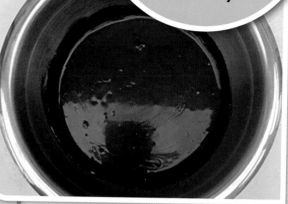

1 Place the sweetened condensed milk into a bowl. Add the chocolate pieces.

2 Ask an adult to boil a pot of shallow water on the stove. Using an oven mitt, place the bowl inside the pot. Stir with a spoon until the chocolate melts completely. Using an oven mitt, take the bowl out of the water and turn off the stove.

3 While the chocolate mixture cools, dust powdered sugar and cornstarch over a clean cutting board or mat. When it is cool enough, pour the chocolate mixture onto the powdered sugar and cornstarch.

4 Using the spoon and your hands, fold the dry ingredients into the chocolate mixture until it is a slime consistency and mixed together well.

47

SMELLY SLIME

Find some soap or candle scents in a craft or hobby store to add a signature aroma to your slime. Will you go for beautifully scented or gross and smelly?

YOU
WILL NEED

Liquid laundry detergent

Liquid soap or candle scent

Food coloring

4 ounces (120 ml) white glue

1 Pour the glue into a large mixing bowl. Add a few drops of food coloring. Mix gently until well combined and the color that you want your slime to be. Try a color that matches the scent you've chosen for your slime (such as green for apple or purple for lavender).

2 Add a few drops of the scent and mix well.

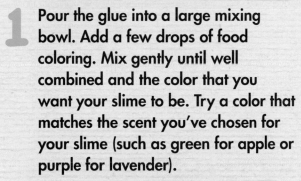

3 Add a small dash of laundry detergent and mix well. Continue mixing in small amounts of laundry detergent until the mixture starts to come off the sides of the bowl.

4 Use your hands to knead the slime mixture until it turns into a slime consistency. Now squish and sniff!

BOUNCING SLIME

Make your very own bouncing ball out of a very basic slime recipe. Keep the recipe simple so the slime comes out thick and more solid than usual.

YOU WILL NEED

Contact solution

Glitter

4 ounces (120 ml) clear glue

Extra Stuff

How many times will your slime ball bounce?

Step by step

1 Pour the glue into a large mixing bowl.

2 Add the contact solution one squirt at a time, mixing it in as you go. Use a spoon until it starts sticking together. Then knead with your hands.

3 Dust some glitter on top of your slime and knead it in.

4 Roll the slime into a ball between the palms of your hands. Now bounce away!

SLIME SUNCATCHER

Wondering what to do with all your cool slime? How about displaying it in the window and letting it catch some sun?!

YOU WILL NEED

A shallow plastic lid (from a food container)

4 or more colors of previously made basic slime (slime made with clear glue is best)

TOP TIP!
Use some vinegar to get the suncatcher off the window later if it gets stuck.

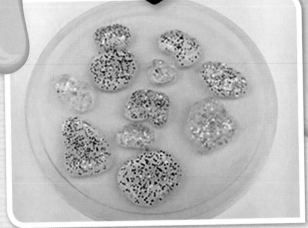

1 Break your slime into small pieces. Place the pieces into the plastic lid, dotting the different colors around each other.

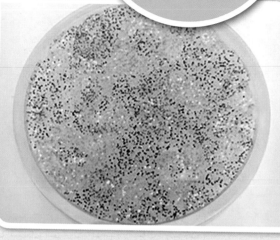

2 Let the slime ooze and settle until it fills all the gaps.

3 Leave the lid flat for three days. As it dries out, the slime should set into one big disc. Peel the disc out of the lid.

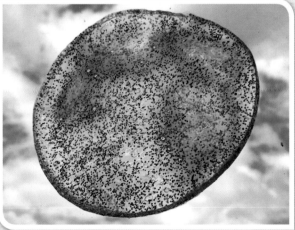

4 Stick your suncatcher on your window and let the light shine through!

HEAT-SENSITIVE COLOR-CHANGING SLIME

A special kind of paint adds a bit of color-changing magic to this slime. Hot or cold, it will let you know!

YOU WILL NEED

Liquid laundry detergent

4 ounces (120 ml) clear glue

Heat-sensitive paint

Try This!

Test out how you can change the slime's color. Dip it into a bowl of cold water or blow hot air on it using a hair dryer. You can even try splitting it in half and making one half cold and the other warm to see the difference!

Step by step

1 Pour the clear glue into a large mixing bowl.

2 Add a generous amount of the paint and mix well. Add more paint until the mixture is the color that you'd like.

3 Add a small dash of laundry detergent and mix well. Continue mixing in small amounts of laundry detergent until the mixture starts to come off the sides of the bowl.

4 Use your hands to knead the slime mixture until it turns into a slime consistency.

55

Want to go beyond making and squishing slime? Try this cool experiment to **BLOW** your mind. Just remember to blow out, not suck in!

YOU WILL NEED

1 batch of basic slime (see pages 14-15)

1 hard plastic straw

Step by step

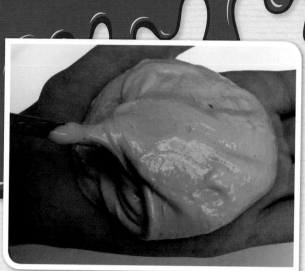

1 Make a batch of basic slime in whatever color you like. For this experiment, don't add too much laundry detergent to your slime—add just enough so that the mixture becomes slime but is only a little stretchy and breaks when pulled apart.

2 Press one end of the straw into the slime.

3 With one hand supporting the slime, take a deep breath and blow into the straw. Watch the slime bubble grow!

NO-GLUE AQUARIUM SLIME

Create a cute little aquarium with simple ingredients from around your house. This slime will be a different consistency than the others, but there's nothing fishy about its fun factor!

YOU WILL NEED

1¼ cups (300 ml) clear or blue shampoo

⅛ tsp (1 g) salt

Small fish-shaped beads

Blue food coloring

1 Squeeze the shampoo into a mixing bowl. Add a few drops of blue food coloring and mix in well.

2 Add the salt. Mix it in carefully. The slime should now be thicker.

3 Place your mixture into a clear container. Add a few fish beads on top.

4 Cover the container and place it in the fridge overnight. When you take it out, the slime will be more solid and jelly-like.

MEGA SLIME

Make a mega slime smoothie by mixing together all your old slimes when you're done with them on their own. This has the ultimate squish factor!

YOU WILL NEED

6 or more small batches of different slimes (the more the better!)

TOP TIP!
If the mixture becomes too stiff, add a little glue. If it's too sticky, add some detergent.

Step by step

TOP TIP!

If you mix the slimes together completely, the colors may merge together and go brown or gray.

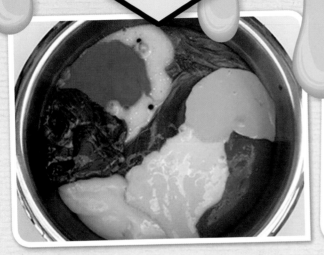

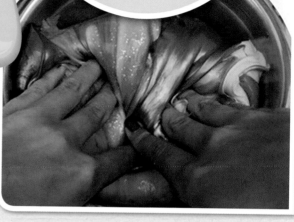

1 Place all your slimes into one very large bowl.

2 With your fingers, gently start folding in the slime from the edges. Mix the slimes together to create different patterns and colors.

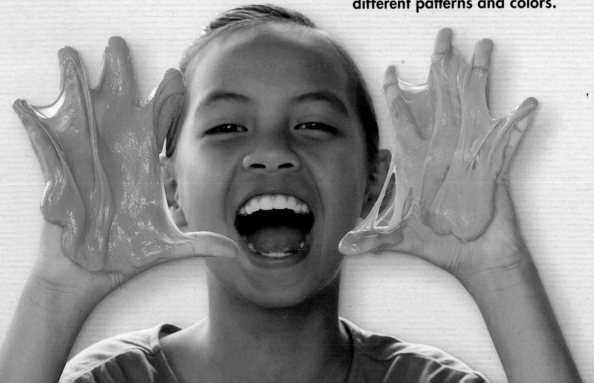

TROUBLESHOOTING

As slime isn't an exact science, things can go wrong or not turn out as you hoped. Never fear...easy fixes are here!

If your slime is...

Too sticky:
Add more activator and knead it in.

Too liquidy:
Add more activator and knead it in.

Too clumpy (and not sticky enovugh):
Add more glue. Mix it in with a spoon and then knead it with your hands when it starts coming off the sides of the bowl.

Not stretchy enough (breaks too easily when pulled apart): Add some lotion and knead it in.

Not coming together:
Be patient! Mix really well after each addition of activator, rather than adding more too quickly, which can turn your slime too hard.

Too hard:
If your slime is starting to go hard from sitting out or being handled too much, run it under tap water. Stretch it out so the water gets absorbed, and then knead in some lotion to the moist mixture.

Too messy:
If slime has ended up in places it shouldn't (like on the carpet or your clothes), use vinegar to dissolve it.

Irritating:
If you find the slime ingredients are irritating your skin due to allergies or eczema, find some protective gloves to wear.

TOP TIP!

If the slime is getting really old (more than a few weeks), smelly (a bad smell that you didn't add in yourself!), or doesn't react to any of these fixes, it's time to throw it out.